the hiss of the viper

the hiss of the viper

Carmelia Leonte

Translated from the Romanian by

Mihaela Moscaliuc

Carnegie Mellon University Press

Pittsburgh 2014

acknowledgments

Much gratitude to the editors of the following journals, in which some of these poems have appeared: *Arts & Letters, Connecticut Review, Connotation Press, Controlled Burn, Great River Review, Hayden's Ferry Review, Kestrel, Maryland Review, Mid-American Review, Mississippi Review, Mosaic, One Trick Pony, Poetry International, Poezia* (Romania), *The Southern California Anthology, Sunscripts, Two Rivers Review.* A number of translations included in this manuscript, some in earlier versions, were published in the chapbook *Death Searches for You a Second Time* (Red Dragonfly Press, 2003).

Special thanks to Michael Waters for his indispensable assistance, to Carmelia Leonte for her trust, and to Monmouth University for support.

Book design by Julia Petrich

Library of Congress Control Number 2014943677
ISBN 978-0-88748-590-9

contents

introduction

In 1998, two years after I came to the United States to pursue graduate work, I returned to Romania to visit family and take my farewell once again. This one would be permanent and, since I could not bring back my family, dowry of colossal down pillows, or my cemetery, I walked into a bookstore and bought all the poetry volumes by authors whose names were unfamiliar to me. I sensed that the way to find a real home in my adopted tongue and stay connected to my native one was through poetry, though I had neither written nor translated poetry before. And I wanted a stranger, just as I was to myself at the beginning of this journey, to accompany me. I winnowed the twenty-some collections down to ten, then five, then to a single chapbook titled *Procesiunea Papuşilor/The Dolls' Procession*, by Carmelia Leonte. A few days later, pure accident brought me to her, though the dismissive introduction her poets-coworkers, all male, had given her (identifying her as a functionary of the Writers House rather than as a writer) made me doubt at first that the woman in front of me was the author whose feisty poems I carried in my pocket. She had not flinched at the introduction.

As I came to know Leonte over the years, I realized that the circumspection and discreetness with which she conducted her life were acts of necessity, both means of protecting writing as a vital source of strength, and an extension of her integrity as a poet attuned to her contemporaries' work, but disinterested in trends, coteries, or accolades. Unlike many of the poets of her generation, who turned to experimentation in the years following the fall of the communist regime, Leonte continued to invest herself in texturing and chiseling her already singular, beautifully quirky voice. In her work, Leonte carves a poetics of literal survival that is concurrently merged into and defiant of the mundane. The poems of *The Hiss of the Viper*, which comprises pieces from three collections, speak of flesh and bone, yet remain somewhat disembodied and haunting. It may be because her poetry serves as a decanter for experiences that discard the sediments of the recognizable personal and seek re-articulation via the symbolic and the mythic. The decanted voices, transpersonal and transtemporal, belong to a richly textured subjectivity, but they steer clear of the confessional mode. In our conversations, Leonte cited the French Symbolists and Emily Dickinson as the most influential predecessors; she also mentioned, somewhat surprisingly, that some of her poems frightened her. "Poems often seem to write *me*, rather than the other way around, and I hope that when they do, they miss some things; if they write me *entirely*—well, that would be tragic."

The poems are dark and prescient, austere and visceral, crystallized and slightly esoteric, resonant with masked social and political critiques and besieged spirituality. Irony and allegory challenge absolutism in its various forms, though the poems do not engage politics overtly. The often addressed "you" takes various forms: God/gods in Christian, pre-Christian, or metaphorical manifestations, lover, doppelgänger, reader, mythological characters, or indefinable interlocutors seduced into listening. Compressed and precise in its lyrical narrative, or ghost of a narrative, a Leonte poem straddles many realms at once.

A poem like "Honeymoon Suite," for instance, places us in a world of Jungian archetypes, myth, and Romanian folklore, a nexus of wedding and funeral, sex and violence, Eros and Thanatos.

Romanian
Camera Nupţială
Lăutarii, dănţuitorii
s-au imbrăcat in negru si te caută.
Eu mă apropii temătoare,
imi sfişii cămasa. Fâşia albă o înmoi
în sînge de şopârlă şi praf de ierburi
ce infloresc o singură dată pe an.
Frumos eşti!
Te dezbraci lent, ceremonial,
iar eu iţi vopsesc trupul.
Te lipeşti de zid.
Forma trupului tău
rămâne in afara ta,
ca un alt trup
pe care îl contempli.

Translation
Honeymoon Suite
The fiddlers, the wedding guests
have put on black clothes and are looking for you.
Nervous, I come near
and tear up my gown. I dip the white rag
in viper blood and crushed herbs
that bloom only once each year.
How handsome you are!
Ceremoniously, you take off your suit
and I paint your flesh.
You press yourself against one wall:
the imprint of your body
stays behind
as if it were someone else
whom you're now just beginning to recognize.

To Romanian readers, the poem will recall, among other
things, the culturally sanctioned violence of an old—and
by now rarely practiced—Romanian ritual: the consumma-

tion of marriage as a community event that involves proof of the bride's virginity. In Leonte's poem, however, the female speaker takes hold of the ritual (as she tears her own gown, dips it in *viper* blood, and "stains" the bridegroom's body), then turns it into a conduit for new knowledge and possible change. The ending of the poem also echoes the famed Romanian ballad of Ana, the walled-up wife who is being sacrificed by her beloved Master Mason Manole for the sake of art (specifically, a monastery that will not stand erect without human sacrifice), a theme to which Leonte returns in "The Walling."

Unfortunately, some cultural references, such as the ones embedded in "Honeymoon Suite," will be lost on English-speaking readers, as will be the partial intranslatability of some Romanian words, such as "lăutarii, dănţuitorii," colloquialisms that evoke, in two words, a familiar aspect of traditional Romanian weddings: the band of virtuosos (often Roma/Gypsies) indispensable to any rites of passage and the devout dancers ("dănţuitorii") who never abandon the dance floor.

When I heard Carmelia read her work aloud in 2000, in her small apartment at the outskirts of Iaşi, I understood why she would see translation as a process of inescapable transformation/deformation of the original. When she gave me free hand to do them justice in English however I saw fit, saying that in another language the poems were not quite hers anymore, I felt both relief and a great deal of anxiety. To a large extent, her poems are meditations on the power of enunciation. For Leonte, the syllable— not the line or the sentence—functions as the integral unit of poetry. Soundwork creates a metalanguage that is as important, if not more important, than content-driven diction. I could not trust my ears alone, just as I could not trust the immigrant, "accented" intimacy I had developed with the English language. The translations would not have been what they are without the exquisite ear and craft of poet Michael Waters, whose input remained invaluable throughout the process. In ferrying these poems into the English, I tried to honor the intensity and seriousness of purpose Leonte brings to the word/world, syllable by syllable.

—Mihaela Moscaliuc

hieroglyph

Do you love me, Death—

the way we hunch together,

your body pressing mine?

Your pulsing eyelid, nervous throbbing,

assure me you'll produce no heir.

Your back and mine, perfectly symmetrical,

recreate a hieroglyph

unearthed in a pyramid generations ago.

Your face and mine, alike and drained,

speak to each other in coded language.

That voice alone betrays you,

how it resonates in my ear:

you will surface as an earthenware bowl

while Death searches for you a second time.

honeymoon suite

The fiddlers, the wedding guests

have put on black clothes and are looking for you.

Nervous, I come near

and tear up my gown. I dip the white rag

in viper blood and crushed herbs

that bloom only once each year.

How handsome you are!

Ceremoniously, you take off your suit

and I paint your flesh.

You press yourself against one wall:

the imprint of your body

stays behind

as if it were someone else

whom you're now just beginning to recognize.

like faith

Look at him! Just when the world becomes unbearable,

he shows up.

His skin's a protective membrane

dividing light from warmth.

One eye laughs,

the other mocks laughter,

two separate creatures

equally seductive.

When heat becomes unbearable,

his skin smolders

like faith.

childhood

The sky clothed us, astonishment stamped on its face.

We awoke: two strangers abandoned and faceless.

What bottomless joy in the eyes

of that creature

shuffling toward us, a blue baby

cradled in both arms.

the gates

With joy I've summoned you here

to witness my parents' heads

impaled on stakes,

ablaze.

To remember their own names,

they posted guards at each

of the hundred gates they passed through.

They were carrying a hundred keys—

the daily count of infamy.

With joy I've summoned you here.

The hundred guards

leap into the fire

one by one.

ways of loving (i)

You lifted yourselves to Heaven and then dove back,

although I've never asked for anything.

You grew petals and you plucked them out,

grew wings and chopped them off,

convinced all these would bring salvation.

You loved one another and birthed children

whom you buried hastily,

etching their names on tiny ivory crosses.

Now you stare me in the face

expecting me to say, humble in my humiliation:

"My brothers, my beloved ones, reach out,

be my crutch, my life,

here, now,

for ever and ever."

ways of loving (iv)

O God, what a long time has passed from yesterday to now.

As if a mountain had collapsed

at the threshold of morning.

As if a plagued town set itself on fire

and we ceremoniously bear our bones through it.

You say you're my father?

If so, why do the silver forks of the orphanage

clang in my pocket?

Are you my bridegroom?

Then where's the tarnished gold of your vow?

I love you, you tell me.

I love you, I reply.

On our shoulders

predatory birds nest.

ways of loving (v)

I can't believe my son took after you.

Your red, gluey flesh

allows no touch.

To you my skin resembles a cape

meant to brighten stone walls, dress bullfighters,

set the crowd aflame,

teach Death a lesson

while beyond me swirl other stone walls, other corridas,

grotesque faces bellowing—

and my son,

why would he take after you?

game

You have a hard time plucking me

from your cupped palm.

Hesitantly, gracefully,

you lower your shadow

onto my back,

dusking me inside,

then swell

my lungs with your breath.

the hiss of the viper

Someone deconstructs your gestures.

Absurd images perpetuate

your absence, the past, our agony.

O, the sibilance of the viper

shuts itself like a book.

When you curve your stacked vertebrae,

halving the air,

the viper abandons the path.

‖

beyond

He bears his vertebrae on his back.

I wonder what spiritual rage drives him,

what joy, what terrible need to push on.

Beyond this, the world—

shining abortion, unpredictable fetus

whose eyes learn how to focus.

Here—the cloud

grown to resemble

a child tormented in the snow.

cloud (i)

The king withdraws in silence.

He's sick, maybe dying.

When the holy days arrive,

he hammers a nail

through the hand that carries the scepter.

cloud (ii)

Wherever you are,

a cross shadows you—

beautiful, white,

almost human,

begging for your soul.

cloud (iii)

As if this were someone else's life,

your palm cups your scalp.

Each dusk,

your fingers worm through,

exhuming the king's crown.

black

The God of Breath has cloaked himself in black.

He carries a book embossed in human skin.

He never opens it—

otherworldly entrails would spill out.

The God of Breath understands that.

He mumbles

the dark march of light.

Life succumbs to transparency.

Salamanders, cursed with divine beauty,

curl back.

The God of Breath understands.

Metamorphosis and petit mal seizures,

the youthful voices and the golden chalice—

they are all in the works.

someone

Someone bursts into your brain

and yells: "Worthless piece of shit!"

Someone slaps you, then runs away.

Morning will never arrive.

Your brother watches as you fall.

Someone casts stones at you.

Someone brands your forehead.

Your curse turns back upon you,

becomes your guillotine.

Someone pretends to love you,

but loathes you.

Someone tells you to keep faith, so you do.

You never suspect the stalker

ready to plant his dagger in your back.

silence

When silence courses through you,

it can't help but resemble death.

Miniature jade figurines contemplate the stillness.

Always,

half of me desires to be

wherever you are,

to bless the golden child,

the wind-up doll from the country of dolls,

to listen to tendons pop through skin

in the crystal manger

over which life and death mimic wise men.

In your presence everything perishes,

king of kings,

wisest of wise men,

always

whole with desire.

the fish world

The inside of the thing takes you to its bone.

The inside of the bone — to another bone,

skeleton of the golden fish.

The fish world!

The female fish have their own gift: they fix the flint
    stone with their eyes

till it sparks alive;

the world turns translucent, the air disappears.

Ecstatic bodies radiate light.

They invent alphabets,

journey through glints,

laugh, sing, devour each other's flesh, resign themselves.

But all these are nothing

in the absence of the King.

God, you have gills!

about the self

Each day, rooms assume the contours

of my body: they circle, lengthen themselves, shrink.

No sweeter victory

than conquering thresholds

and windows

in the space's erotic courting

of its Self.

the walling

Why do I seek canonization within walls

now that the masonry's done?

What smooth rope pulls me

inside the body of this brick?

The symphony thrashed its skull in my belly,

following the Creator's command:

Survive.

wounds

You were all wounds replenished with rainwater,

your body an oasis for wild beasts.

Grief or death was stripping the bark from ancient oaks.

I circled frantically

        for the path out of the woods—

flag

If our gestures weren't so slow

as to make time toss us toward its edge,

if we didn't get slapped even by our own dreams,

this scream I've wrapped around me like a flag

would be softer, more callow than death.

passage

You swim through light, searching.

The fact that you don't recognize me

when I transmute into scream

suggests you'll find pleasure only in death.

Despair: a ballroom

where no one can find a partner.

Despair: an autumn

where treetops strangle each other.

Where are you?

My days have braided

into a strident season

—no one's—

and no one can remember

the light that once flooded its face.

prayer

My blood's cadenced like prayer.

I hear it throbbing through arteries:

Christ must be praying.

I knew this was coming.

I cross myself

and listen:

sap bleeding through the wooden cross.

communion

The faithless dumb gawk

at the great communion.

The dead and the living

—in all guises—

commingle,

reconcile.

Warm breeze—

life resembles you.

The most recent future

shakes you off its shoulders,

then victory chews your earlobe

before lifting you

from speechlessness.

doubt

How sad they were, lumbering toward me,

the army of moribund priests

with torn habits and hearts split four ways,

the wasteland brandished on their faces,

and no one bothering to let them through—

murmur

Enough, enough, pale murmur.

The fire has caught.

The ants come after us,

cruel army

for whom death

is only a problem of space.

stay

If the inside of the moon were

a transparent egg

through which we could watch moon and moonlight,

if the egg housed

both bird and light,

the moon would break through the eggshell,

eyes chuckle, foreheads ripple.

Night would destroy its monsters,

you'd take my place, and here you'd nest.

apocalypse

A bird, its human carcass

crouched under the feather coat,

a bird, its one eye

open forever

so I can gaze

inside her

while she gazes out:

here's the apocalypse.

light

The sun's child pulls me into light.

Eyes don't hurt, bones do.

These bones—the skeleton

of an ancient instrument

unearthed from stone, fractured, splintered,

sucked up into the light.

Witness to the final deception.

Death sonorous, abstract,

of infinite breadth.

The sun's child is laughing.

He's invented a tale whose ending

has just been made irrelevant.

initiation

The neophyte's delirium, mildewed void,

gives the body's secret away.

The young stride fiercely, clip off

their tongues, like St. Maximus the Confessor.

No room for betrayal.

Neither bitter waters

nor the deserts below the earth

believe that love starts by confessing its deed.

Face to face,

you restore the memory of your kin,

the kin who don't exist.

Where are the pipe dreamers?

Nameless,

hauling their houses on frail backs under the scorching sun,

they stride fiercely,

bodies contorted with youthfulness.

motionless

If you were the Death-Bird,

I would remain motionless,

imagining the worlds you see,

until my stillness

mimicked

that unattainable horizon in your eye.

the flight

You wanted me to dwell in the shadows of your inverted eyes.

No! I screamed, shielding my eyes.

Such infinite sadness froze the cranes' flight westward.

Imaginary, impassible snows buried their rotting corpses.

testament

I, the King,

offer you my feline skin,

the golden hooves of the horses

who have brought me to you,

the black cart of childhood,

the crucifix, the crystal ears

filled with a perfectly vertical howl

in the afternoon of the Messiah—

this insistent version of ourselves.

Shielded by your cloak,

guilt-stricken,

you must steal away from my palace.

motherland

In this nightmare you can no longer recall

who conquered what.

The motherland is a fortress

holding you captive,

cradling you within her river slabs.

The King, lost in no-man's-land,

crawls under your garments, under your skin.

He's shivering. Crying.

Like a pack of howling dogs,

the motherland chases you.

No one has immersed you in the holy waters

mentioned in books. No one.

In your stillness you become

the slow dimming of a streak of light.

The motherland slides her cold fingers

over your porous skin.

the mother

The child's mother is yellow and in tears.

You can walk through her

as if through a ball of wax.

She does not plead. She leaves no traces.

She's grinding one thought alone:

Teach me obedience.

The sun's child is laughing again.

Beware him in his laughter.

autumn landscape

Mother steps over me, thinking I'm dead. She covers me with a sheet, walks out of the room, dozes off on the other side of the door. When she falls asleep, I open my eyes, throw off the sheet. I look around. Mother thinks I am dead. I push the walls aside, push Mother aside, step into her dream, say: "I have resurrected, Mother. Wake up."

Mother gets up, grabs the knife, wants to slash my veins. I let her cut them, then I step out of her dream, push the wall back, push Mother back, slip back under the sheet.

Everything is fine. Mother is asleep, and I am still convinced I am dead.

insomnia, insomnia (i)

At dusk the gravedigger finds himself weeping

anyone is anyone else and no one is himself

dead queens lie on immense sarcophagi

I kneel before them but for what   for whom?

In a tree stump there's an old man with a bugle

through him my insomnia seeps into the earth

cold and crazed we're waiting, as always, for some disaster

I kneel before You but for what   for whom?

It's morning within us a tragic morning

wild creepers entwine our bodies

at dusk the gravedigger finds himself weeping

anyone is anyone else and no one is himself

insomnia, insomnia (ii)

I feel trapped inside myself as in a foreign town

each morning a bird lifts my eyelids

(afflicted by phthisis or just melancholy?)

then leads me like a blind man among objects

Today I'm older than on the day I'll die

I reinvent my features with childish pleasure

then hunt down my brother's eye anticipate him

whispering: *you have become translucent*

We stray among objects wary yet indifferent

scorched wings bandage my eyes

how untraceable we are to ourselves how lost

like one raindrop caught in a wrinkle on Death's face

repentance

The Greek god stores his garments

in a trunk made of human skin.

You locked the trunk yourself—

a scream through clenched teeth.

Don't move. Any movement

could unsettle the world beyond.

The Greek god keeps silent.

He cannot reveal the past

of blood and language.

His sword falls. The world flashes.

Memory. Repentance.

Would it be different if

this petrified face belonged to someone else?

merging colors

You pried me out of Greece's belly

as if I were fungus,

you halved my face, turned it

into the garbled dictum of a hermetic poet

and gathered minstrels to souse me in songs

woven out of love and death,

exile and resurrection.

My shroud's aflame

with hunger,

but they shut me

down.

I have learned to live by laundering language:

smoothed into filaments of silk,

I feign eternal sleep.

I have learned to live by hating poets.

I know nothing of death:

a pseudo-word

spindling from your eyes

sliced in mid-utterance?

Maybe I should start loving.

the testimony of phaedra

The laws you've buried in others

return to you.

The fireball is a law.

I touch the cold ivory and realize:

the left half of your skull overshadows the right.

You seem a hideous child crying out his name

between bellows of laughter.

How could I be more, when halved.

The memory of the room coils into itself. It tightens

around us like a corset of fear,

a chastity belt.

phaedra, on hippolytus

Like a red medusa,

your head fixes my eyes,

absorbs me.

On the inside—the brain, seed of light,

a plant swallowing its fruit.

On the outside—

brightness

without its scream.

You're still alive,

but lost in light

as in a glass coffin

to which they all wish you.

Your good fortune: the other.

hippolytus's confession

Through liquid temples, the angel of love yearns

for its shape,

which has been lost in sound. You're a bustard

whose yellow wings sprout from your hair, incessant

fluttering

that makes me believe you're approaching.

Through you, torture names itself.

Life on one side, and on the other,

the very proof of your existence.

Who will want me when you turn

your tortured face away,

perfectly still?

hippolytus, on himself

The earth bears too little fruit

and keeps squinting,

as if carrying the burden of all things

on its eyelids.

Too harsh a light.

The memory of the Great Priest

cuts through me.

Perhaps the world, however small,

boasts a tender monster

that copies us,

a monster far too young

who loves illusions

the way the fetus loves the placenta,

the way skin hangs onto bone,

desperately.

avatar

Disease and irreverence

have buried you to the knees

in festering soil.

Black flight,

snake clout,

knees hungering for victory.

Seize your thoughts.

Shiny like a mercenary,

the scream takes the shape

of love's ailing body.

O, love,

god whose two faces

sink their teeth into each other

till they bleed,

insomnia of the moment,

pitiful levitation,

sluggishness.

Seize yourselves.

Shiny, timorous, tentative.

You are buried to the waist, to your shoulders,

in the flesh of this future's future.

Beauty, stout love,

you pleasure vipers

with your fungi.

Black flight,

mutiny,

gods sentenced to eternal avatars.

the civilization of forgiveness

The skies closed shop.

The temple's high priestess

stares every pagan

in the eye,

as if she were an image

that can make all heads turn at once.

She wants to spot the guilty one

so she can forgive him.

The civilization of absolution will soon arrive,

she prophesizes,

and I will stretch my coppery arms

over the tormented.

From deep below, deliberate

as a coral reef, the guilty one

emerges.

The priestess seizes him with her mind's eye,

experiences as her own his contorted bones.

Quiet.

The sea throws her nets over the shore,

corals keep afloat in the distance.

hypnosis

Before knowing you,

I knew the mask Medusa

dropped at the gate to the fortress.

Dream in a dream doubling as sleep,

doubling its power to hold the spell.

I descended into a sea of scarlet shells.

They slashed my skin, cutting down to the bone,

bone of an undying master.

Padlocked within light, padlocked within light.

agamemnon, about lost bones (ii)

I had allowed myself to be creaturely,

to descend, gather waters,

shoulder them up into streams.

I had lugged clay amphora

as if I were a yoked beast.

But what a healer I was!

My presence turned worlds

into deserts.

Even the tree in front of my house,

erect as lava, convulses into waves.

Do not draw near!

Within my searing view,

feral children shed their skin.

This tree's discarded soul, the almost-touch,

this longing, its melancholy—

I was swaying, pulled by gravity,

and pretended to be dancing in the embrace of tentacles,

a child in adult mask

watching over the tower of green, dreamy bones.

My love has never been this intense.

I watched his thorny wreath, the joys of exclusion.

I learned to watch him in the dark

lest I might touch and wake him,

and I was his dream, surging from below, a sphere.

text

Green, weedy blood

scrawls the page written to no one.

Her love:

dormant magma

in which you wash your hands.

Each character resembles the weeping of the nun

who genuflects

at the sight of the bridegroom.

The living on one side,

the offspring of the living on the other,

and the past,

smothering them all.

carmelia leonte is the author of four volumes of poetry (*Procesiunea Păpuşilor/The Dolls' Procession; Melancolia Pietrei/The Melancholy of Stones; Graţia Viespilor/The Gracefulness of Wasps*, which was awarded the Writers' Union Prize; and the bilingual collection *Fiul Sunetului/The Son of Sound*), a collection of travel essays (*La umbra lui Don Quijote/In the Shadow of Don Quixote*), a children's book, reviews, and translations from the work of Marguerite Duras. She has been awarded residency fellowships in Switzerland, Greece, Spain, and Belgium. She lives in the city of Iaşi, in northern Romania, and works as editor for the Press of Literary Museums.

mihaela moscaliuc is the author of *Father Dirt* (Alice James Books, 2010) and *Immigrant Model* (University of Pittsburgh Press, 2015), and the recipient of a 2011 Glenna Luschei *Prairie Schooner* Award and a 2012 Artist Fellowship Award from the New Jersey Arts Council. Her poems, translations, reviews, and articles appear in *The American Poetry Review, The Georgia Review, New Letters, Prairie Schooner, TriQuarterly, Arts & Letters, Mississippi Review, Connecticut Review*, and *Orient and Orientalisms in US-American Poetry and Poetics*. She is assistant professor of English at Monmouth University and teaches in the low-residency MFA Program at Drew University.